ALEX ASKS GRANDPA ABOUT THE OLDEN DAYS

A 1940s Story

Gary L. Wilhelm

Alex Asks Grandpa About the Olden Days: A 1940s Story

Copyright ©2019 Gary Wilhelm

US Government Copyright Office RegistrationTX-8-816-062

Illustrator Pieter Els

Compiler Carolyn Wilhelm

All rights reserved.

No part of this book may be reproduced, stored in a retrieval system or transmitted by any means without the written permission of the author.

ISBN: 9781729375280

Imprint: Wise Owl Factory LLC Maple Grove, MN 55369

9813 Zinnia Lane North, Maple Grove, MN 55369

Library of Congress Control Number:2019917404

Additional Credits
Two illustrations from Deposit Photos (Skunk, Bull Silhouette)
Book design © 2017, BookDesignTemplates.com (adapted by C. Wilhelm)
Images for stories at the end of the book:
Haircut story
https://depositphotos.com/4464567/stock-photo-barbers-pole-and-sky-room.html
Pheasant story
https://pixabay.com/photos/nature-wildlife-outdoors-grass-3341419/
Milk can story
https://pixabay.com/photos/milk-milk-cans-pot-agriculture-2612122/
Mayme Wilhelm story
Family photo (scanned)
Windmill story
https://depositphotos.com/13804542/stock-photo-old-windmill.html

Dedicated to:

All Grandparents Everywhere

and

My Wilhelm Family (you know who you are)

Contents

Alex Asks Grandpa About the Olden Days 1

The Bull 20

The Skunk Story 36

About the Author 62

About the Illustrator 63

Early Haircuts in Faulkton 64

Pheasant Hunting in South Dakota 66

A Milk-can Full of Cash 68

Mayme Wilhelm 70

Wind-farm early 1900's Style 74

Alex Asks Grandpa About the Olden Days

Alex asked, "Are we going to Grandpa's? May I ask him about the olden days?"

"Yes," said Mom. "He knows you are going to ask him. I know you like the stories he tells."

The first thing Alex said was hello when he saw his Grandpa. Then right away, he asked, "What do you remember about your house when you were growing up, Grandpa?"

"We lived in a small white house with a metal roof located in a town of about 1,000 people in South Dakota. There were two stories and an unfinished basement. Coal was burned in a basement furnace to provide heat in the winter. There was no air conditioning…only open windows and fans. On the first floor there was a living room, two very small bedrooms, a small kitchen, and a bathroom. Upstairs were two bedrooms and a storage room. There was an attached shed on the back of the house that leaked when it rained. In the back yard was a vegetable garden."

"We lived there with my Mother's parents, my town Grandma and Grandpa. Three generations lived there. Grandpa would sometimes play his fiddle. I remember him playing 'Red River Valley' and everyone would sing. I liked that."

"In the winter, a special treat was home-made ice cream! We would get cream from a farm. The cream was mixed with other ingredients and put into the inner container of a hand-cranked ice cream maker. Ice chopped from a nearby lake, and a bit of salt, was added between the inner container and the outer wall. Then we turned the crank which rotated the inner container until the ice chilled the ingredients, thus causing them to thicken, and become ice cream. This ice cream was a special treat . . . at Christmas."

Grandpa explained, "One thing that was different was that we had a wooden phone hanging on the wall. I remember it had a crank lever, and the local 'operator' connected us to other phones from a switchboard. It was a party line and other people could listen in on calls made."

"That was your phone, Grandpa? Other people could listen to what you said? Was it a smartphone?" Alex asked.

"No, it only allowed talking and listening. There were no apps. The phones did not have videos or games on them."

"What did you do without apps? Did you watch television?" Alex wondered.

"We didn't have a television. We had a radio in a large cabinet, and I liked to listen to the adventure stories of the Lone Ranger," answered Grandpa.

"You just listened? There was no video?"

"Yes," answered Grandpa. "Just like you are listening to my story right now, only out of the radio's speaker."

"Oh. Was the Lone Ranger a story?" asked Alex.

"Oh, yes, the Lone Ranger was a cowboy with a horse. There was a new story each week," explained Grandpa.

"That sounds fun. And I wonder, did you have a grandma and grandpa?" Alex asked. "I have six."

"I had two grandmas and two grandpas," answered Grandpa. "Town Grandma and Grandpa, and farm Grandma and Grandpa. Town Grandma would often read to me...various series of books from the library, such as the Hardy Boys, Nancy Drew Mysteries, Lone Ranger, and so on. I really liked that."

"Farm Grandpa and Grandma lived about three miles east of town and two miles north. The road north was so bad that it was impassible whenever it rained. I think it was just a dirt road...not even gravel," Grandpa remembered.

Grandpa also remembered, "The farmhouse had a big cooking stove in the kitchen near the front entrance. There was a bin filled with corncobs nearby. They burned corncobs and some wood in the stove to cook and heat the house. On the porch there was a hand-cranked separator to remove cream from the cow's milk. A wooden butter churn was also kept on the porch. Water was carried to the house from the well in pails. The bathroom was an outhouse with no running water. It was located about 50 feet from the house."

"During winter blizzards, a rope was used from the house to barn to go feed the animals in the barn, and make it back to the house without becoming disoriented by the blinding snow."

Alex wondered if there were animals on the farm.

"Yes," answered Grandpa. "During summer there were chickens running loose in the farmyard. There were also cows and pigs on the farm. The barn had a haymow, where hay was stored for feeding the cows in winter. There were also two large workhorses named Tom and Jerry, on the farm. There was another horse for riding to the one-room country school, several miles away."

The Bull

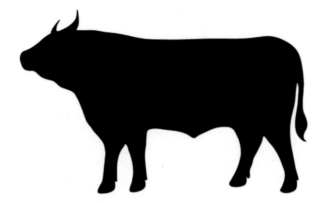

"In fact, one of the animals on the farm was a bull. This is a little story for you from when I was younger than you are, now," said Grandpa.

"One time when I was very young, I was visiting grandpa and grandma's farm near Faulkton, for the afternoon. They took me to the barn and told me that there was a young bull in one of the stalls. They said stay away from that stall, because bulls can be aggressive."

"Does aggressive mean they could get mad, Grandpa?"

"Yes, that is what it means. Later in the afternoon, I was up in the hay loft...the second story of the barn. There was hay up there for feeding the animals in the stalls below. This was done through holes in the floor above each stall. These feeding holes were about two feet square. Hay was shoveled through these holes to the animals below."

"I was walking around up in the hay loft, and did not notice some hay was covering one of the feeding holes. I tried walking there, and of course the hay gave way, and I tumbled down the feeding hole. And guess where I landed? On the head of the young bull, who had been enjoying his lunch of fresh hay."

"Oh, no!" said Alex. "Ouch!"

"I'm not sure who was more surprised: the bull or me? As soon as I saw where I was, I jumped down, slid through the boards of the stall, and got out of there as fast as I could. I'm not sure how the bull reacted. He probably wondered what this was the fell out of the sky and landed on his head. Or maybe he thought he had taken a bite of bad hay or something...who knows."

"Were you in trouble, Grandpa?"

"I do not think so. Anyway, I was very glad to escape without being injured, and much more careful when walking in the hay loft from then on."

Speaking of animals, Grandpa said, "Every spring cartons of chicks would arrive at the post office for the farmers who had ordered them. When you went to the post office then, you would hear all these chicks peeping."

"Peep! Peep!"

"Yes, just like that, Alex."

"When they were younger," Grandpa continued, "farm Grandma and Grandpa would get together for barn dances with some of the neighbors. They would all bring food and have a dance in someone's barn."

Grandpa also recounted, "Dance music was provided by farmers playing their instruments."

I've never danced in a barn, thought Alex. In fact, I haven't been to a barn at all!

Grandpa said pumpkin patches are small farms, and told Alex he has been to pick pumpkins.

"Oh, I have been to a small farm, then!" remembered Alex.

"In the fall there was a lot of manual labor involved in harvest time, at the farm when the crops were ready. The grain was put in 'shocks' by hand. Sometimes a traveling harvest crew would come through the area with a large threshing machine, powered via a long, wide belt, from the engine on a nearby steam tractor."

"Did you help?" asked Alex.

"I was too young to help," answered Grandpa.
"I was only about your age."

"I saw a threshing crew with their big steam-powered machine only once…it was a sight to behold! If the work crew stayed for several days, they were allowed to sleep in the barn on the straw, and farm Grandma made food for them."

Steam-powered Threshing Machine

A large black steam-tractor with huge iron wheels would be parked adjacent to the threshing machine. The steam engine on the tractor supplied power to the threshing machine via a long belt that was nearly one foot wide.

"Farm Grandma also did a lot of work in the fall, canning vegetables to preserve them for use in winter."

"I like vegetables!" said Alex.

"I know you do. That is good!" said Grandpa.

Grandpa thought a minute and continued talking. He said, "I believe one of my Dad's first jobs was unloading railroad cars full of grain using a scoop shovel; however during most of Dad's life he had his own independent excavation business and he was very proud of that. Dad was also a County Commissioner for many years."

The Skunk Story

"I have a skunk story for you. Do you want to hear it?"

"Yes! Was the skunk stinky?"

"Well . . . let me think."

Grandpa started the story.

"I have a vivid memory of a trip to a farm when my Dad was trying to collect payment for excavation work he had done for the farmer."

"My Mom, Dad, and I were in the car and we drove into the farmer's yard. I was sitting on Mom's lap. Dad got out of the car and went over to talk with the farmer."

"Meanwhile, a small boy came up to our side of the car. He was probably about 5 or 6 years old, with ragged clothes and a dirty face. He said 'Dad shot a skunk; we cooked it; and boy was it good!' I suppose I remember this because Mother was quite mortified."

"My Dad was not able to collect his money...we left the farm and went home. Economic conditions in Faulk County were not very good back then, but we didn't know anybody ate skunk."

"That was a sad story!" exclaimed Alex. "I didn't know that one."

"Yes, I agree, very sad." said Grandpa.

Grandpa continued remembering the olden days. He said, "The Faulkton Record was the local newspaper. It was located in a building on Main Street containing a large linotype machine, which produced castings or lead slugs for letters and punctuation type for the paper."

"I was a paper-boy for a different paper and mowed lawns. That reminds me of my other job. For six years, I was a projectionist at the local movie theater, to earn money."

"Because they didn't have videos then?" Alex wondered.

"That's right!" Grandpa answered.

"Our town had at least one train depot agent who still communicated by telegraph using Morse Code; a series of short and long sounds. I remember being in the depot and hearing him tap out messages."

Alex asked, "When was this, again?"
Grandpa said, "In the 1940s and 1950s."

"Was that about a hundred years ago?"

"Not quite," laughed Grandpa.

"My Dad was very generous to the town with his construction business. Every new church, lodge hall, or other community building had excavation provided free by Dad. He also contributed free work to the golf course and swimming pool."

"That was nice! I like to swim!" exclaimed Alex.

"Swimming is good exercise," said Grandpa.

"Johnny-the-blacksmith had a shop in town," Grandpa explained.

"A blacksmith is a person who makes and repairs things made of iron, by hand. Johnny really liked kids and would help repair their bikes for free. I remember his forge, anvil, and hot coals. He would work on the farmers' plowshares by heating them until they glowed. Then he would beat on them with a hammer to reshape them, and grind until sharp."

"That sounds like hard work!" Alex shared.

"Yes, it was very hard," agreed Grandpa.

"What did your mother do?" asked Alex.

"My Mother was busy teaching at her country school, but that was not very much pay…especially in those days. Later, my Mother served on the Faulkton School Board for a number of years. Mother was also active in church and several clubs."

"Your Mother was a teacher? My Mother is a teacher, too!" said Alex. "There are teachers at my school."

"Just down the street from my house was a garage where they fixed cars," said Grandpa. "The family who owned it lived upstairs over it with their 13 children. One of the children was my age and was a close friend. I learned some things about car repair from visiting there and other local garages, although I didn't work on my own cars until many years later."

"Like when you changed the tire that time!" Alex stated.

"My Dad would take me fishing from the shore. We used bamboo poles at first. He would clean the fish and we would eat it. A few years later he got a boat. He would take the townspeople for rides on the local lake on the 4th of July. When I was older, I drove the boat and helped too, on that holiday. Later we had rods and reels for fishing. Dad became known around town as a really good fisherman. He liked to fish for bass and walleyes."

"I like fish!" said Alex.

"That is good!" said Grandpa.

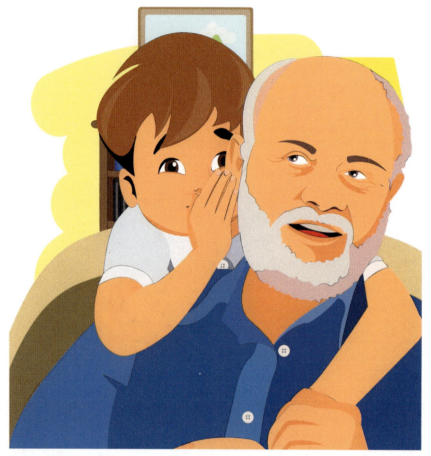

"Will you tell me more someday, Grandpa? You tell amazing stories," whispered Alex.

"I have many stories, Alex, and I'm sure I have more to tell you!" answered Grandpa. "Thank you for asking."

About the Author

Gary L. Wilhelm is a retired engineer with a master's degree from South Dakota State University, who did research and development work in America, Asia, and Europe for consumer, commercial, and military products, during a career of several decades. In addition to being a civilian engineer embedded with the Marines during the Vietnam War in 1968 and 1969, he worked developing products ranging from EF Johnson citizens band radio, and the Texas Instruments home computer, communications technology for use within buildings, and with medical devices implanted within the body, to the Howitzer Improvement Program (HIP) for army artillery on the battlefield. He was also a representative on a North Atlantic Treaty Organization (NATO) committee. He hosted the USA meeting of the committee at Honeywell.

He is happily married to Carolyn with a daughter Betsy and son Michael. He likes being a Grandpa!

His first book was *Good Afternoon Vietnam: A Civilian in the Vietnam War.*

https://gary-l-wilhelm-author.com/

About the Illustrator

Pieter Els has 30+ years of experience in facilitating courses to junior and senior facilitators, learning aids development, course material development, and marketing and web design. At first, he has earned a Graphic Design Diploma and during his career, as well as several merit bonuses for outstanding educational services and products. Later in his career he decided to also get his BTech Degree in Graphic Design. Some of the other qualifications he obtained were: Educational Technology (EDTECH) Facilitator, Learning Aids Developer, Learning Material Developer and Assessor. He also took several courses in Computer Based Training, E-learning Software and attended Middle and Senior Management Courses. One of his major responsibilities later in his career was the research on distance learning.

Pieter has an online resource company for education clip art, illustrations, tutorials and articles. His company goal is to offer the world of education more high-quality art and learning materials. Surfer Kids Clip Art was established on Christmas Day, December 25, 2013

He is happily married to Elizabe with a daughter Nika and son Eswan.

Pieter Els
Surfer Kids Clip Art
Jeffreys Bay
South Africa
www.surferkiddies.com
surferkidsclipart@gmail.com

Early Haircuts in Faulkton

G. Wilhelm July-2018

There was one single chair barber shop in town, and my earliest memory is of a middle-aged barber named Nystrom...I think his first name was Eric.

My mother would give me money (50 cents I think) and have me walk the two blocks alone, up town to the village barber to get my hair cut. After paying the barber, he would give me a nickel back for my own personal use...such a deal! Actually a nickel would buy something in the 1940's. There was usually conversation in the barber shop... between customers and with the barber...topics such as the weather, crop prices, one upmanship, and yes, gossip.

I remember one such haircut. On this day there were no other customers, just the barber Eric and me. Near the end of the haircut, Eric explained to me how difficult it

was to make a living...with his hands simply cutting hair. His hands had to make all his money to live. The barber shop had an open
window. A fan was blowing cool air, and shade from the sun was provided inside the shop.

After I paid, at the end of my haircut, Eric asked if it would be OK for him to give me an old pair of his scissors instead of a nickel this time? OK, anything to help out. Guess what...I still have the scissors and they have been useful. That was a very good deal for me!

Pheasant Hunting in South Dakota
G. Wilhelm December 2020

The ring-necked pheasant was imported to America from Asia. Pheasants were introduced to South Dakota in 1898, and thrived especially in central SD. The males have colorful plumage including a bright white neck ring. The females are gray. The meat from pheasants is delicious...somewhat like chicken, but better. Pheasants need weedy fence rows, crop land, or bushy woods for escape cover. Pheasant hunting season was in October every year...it often started on October 19, which was my father's birthday.

My Wilhelm grandparents (along with other farm families) would host out-of-state hunters each year. The hunters would come for about a week at the beginning of hunting season and stay at my grandparent's farmhouse. My grandmother would cook for them, and they would hunt during the day. As I recall there were 6 of them. One of these, an MD, came from Hawaii every year; I believe the others were from the eastern states. There was no set price; they just all contributed, and my grandparents did well. This started in the late 1940's continued for several years even after my grandparents retired from farming, and moved into town.

One type of hunting was road-hunting, where hunters would drive along a country road until they saw a white ring-neck in the fence row. They would then stop the car, get out. If they were good sportsmen, they would walk over to flush the bird and give it a chance to fly before they tried to shoot it in flight. Others would just shoot the pheasant on the ground. My grandfather, who had a sense of humor, would sometimes take a ring-necked pheasant head and put it, clearly visible, on a short stick in the fence row, for a good laugh at the expense of some hunter.

A Milk-can Full of Cash
G. Wilhelm November 2020

After entrepreneur, Phil Findeis died in 1960, my grandparents received an unusual request: to help his wife search the nooks and crannies of his house and business for cash that she knew had been hidden there over the years because they did not trust the banks, after what had happened in the depression of the 1930's. She knew many dollars had been hidden over the years, but didn't remember exactly where it all was. She knew my grandparents as customers, and knew of their reputation for integrity and paying their bills. My grandparents were asked to help her locate all this cash that had been stashed over many years.

Phil Findeis as born in Germany, and came to the USA in 1885. He settled in Miranda, a town smaller that Faulkton...a few miles East and a few miles South of Faulkton. Miranda was also located on a railroad, which was important for his business there.

Phil started out managing the Miranda Elevator for Atlas Company. But he soon began his own business enterprises. He sold lumber and hardware, machinery and most necessities. He brought all this to Miranda by rail. Then the farmers would come to Miranda to get it. He also bought livestock and used the railroad to transport it to its destination. Farmers for miles around would buy a railroad car of fence from Phil to fence off their farms. For a time, Phil even became a manufacturer of cement blocks. He and his wife Ella ran the business very successfully until Phil died in 1960. They were model citizens, known and respected throughout the area.

My grandparents and Phil's wife searched and as they found cash, they put it in a milk can. (A can about a foot in diameter and 2 1/2 feet tall). When the several day search was complete it was full of cash...approximately $20,000.00 in all.

Mayme Wilhelm
G. Wilhelm July 2017

Amy May Zaelke was born July 11, 1906 in Faulkton, South Dakota...a town of about 800 people. For most of her life she was known as Mayme. Her father had a plumbing and heating business in Faulkton. Both of her parents were involved in many community organizations. Her mother was especially active in women's rights issues and in creating a library for the town and county. Mother attended grades 1-12 in Faulkton.

The Picklers were one of the prominent families in Faulkton at this time. Because Mother's mother was a close friend of Mrs. Pickler, there was a coming-out party for Mother at the Pickler Mansion in or around 1924. (Yes, a debutante ball for Mother at a mansion in Faulkton, S.D.) The John and Alice Pickler home on the south edge of Faulkton is a prairie Victorian home featuring 20 rooms in three stories. The home was used to host many visiting dignitaries including Susan B. Anthony, who stayed with them three times, Teddy Roosevelt, and Grover Cleveland. I wonder if grandma Zaelke met Susan B. Anthony during these visits; I have no way of knowing for sure. However I knew grandma Zaelke, and I am certain she would have worked for women's suffrage. She was also a member of the W.C.T.U. John Pickler had been a major in the civil war, and was known as Major. He was elected four times to represent South Dakota at-large in the United States House of Representatives, serving from 1889 to 1897. He and his wife Alice promoted women's suffrage and were friends with Susan B Anthony. The will-bequeathed wish of Alice Pickler that the house be made into a community museum, became a reality in 1988, and it is now available for tours.

Mother attended Northern State College in Aberdeen and finished a two-year teaching certificate. At that time only a two-year certificate was required to teach. At that time, the only teaching job she could get was in a one room country school. She then began teaching grades 1-8 in a school near Faulkton. She taught all subjects and also took care of cleaning the school building as well, with some help from the students. The un-insulated building was heated by a coal burning stove. Those close to the stove were overheated; those away from the stove were cold. There was no running water. She was responsible for everything including music, physical education, special school programs for the parents...with the exception of snow removal. I attended her school Christmas program in 1964. The program was very good and the parents seemed impressed. The schools were managed by township boards. They determined teacher salary...which was very low, and no benefits. She once fell on ice on the school steps. Her knee was damaged and required surgery. She asked the township to pay for the medical bills, as they were responsible for snow and ice removal. They resisted and I'm not sure whether they paid or not. I once asked her why at some point, she didn't try to get a teaching job in Faulkton, where George, Gloria, and I went to school. She replied that she preferred the multi-grades, liked being independent, and wanted to avoid politics with other teachers.

On September 3, 1931 Mayme Zaelke and Clarence Wilhelm were married. It was a double wedding in Redfield, S.D.; the other couple were Ted Paulson and Bertha Stickney. Mother and Dad had a son named Clair, who was born with birth defects on July 5 and died after only a few months in 1932. Clair is buried in Faulkton Cemetery with only an evergreen tree marking the grave. Dad and Mother were left with medical bills and their car was repossessed. This was during the Great Depression. Times were hard and they really struggled. In 1936, they moved in with Mother's parents and shared expenses and their home. Mother continued teaching and Dad found available work...mostly physical labor and other odd jobs, I think.

I (Gary) was born April 26, 1943 in Faulkton Hospital...a building constructed of stones, located across the street from our house. Dad had been drafted to help fight WWII and was away in the Navy. I believe Mother continued to teach until Gloria (1947) and George (1949) were born. Dad started a small excavation business in 1947 and Mother became a stay-at-home mother. Mother was a member of Tuesday Club, the Rebekah Lodge, and other community organizations. Tuesday Club of Faulkton was organized in 1897 as a literary club exclusively for ladies, who were teachers or retired teachers. The club goal was to stimulate intellectual and social culture among its members. The Rebekah's are a Fraternal as well as a service organization and are associated with the Odd Fellows Lodge. At the urging of other community members who respected her knowledge of education, she served on the Faulkton School Board for a number of years while she was a stay-at-home mother.

We attended the Congregational Church and I think that helped Mother through the tough times. She was very active in the church and held several positions there. For a while in the 1950's Mother even took a correspondence course to qualify as a minister. I believe the course was through a place called Unity out of Lee Summit, Missouri. Her lessons were hand written, and I remember taking their thick envelopes to mail at the post office. I don't believe she finished it...probably lack of money.

I think, more than anything else, there was one thing Dad did that made things tough for Mother and the rest of us; that was he drank. Dad would leave for work in the morning, and he would sometimes not come home at night, and maybe not the next night or two. There was no way of knowing where he was or even if he was ever coming back. This happened for decades and I don't know how she survived this...maybe religion? I have often wondered: why did Dad drink and disappear? Was it alcoholism, cronyism, depression, something else, or a combination of all these things?

In spite of this, he did build and run a business for more than 25 years, and was a County Commissioner for a number of years.

After staying home for years with us kids Mother's teaching license had lapsed. In the late 1950's Mother spent a summer car-pooling two hours a day, every weekday from Faulkton to Aberdeen for class, to renew her teaching certificate so she could resume teaching in one room country schools. I think some money was needed to help with family expenses. She did teach more years, and ended her teaching career teaching at the Blumengard Hutterite Colony 20 miles north of Faulkton. This Hutterite teaching was once again a one room school situation. The Hutterites prevented her from teaching certain things. I'm not exactly sure when her teaching career ended, but it was in the 1960's. After teaching a total of 25 years, her starting pension was $22 per month...and she really looked forward to the day it arrived. She worked long and hard as a dedicated teacher, in addition to being an active community member, a mother, and a wife. Mother was especially happy to have all of her children home for holidays. Mother made home-made ice cream using ice from the lake, did baking, had fudge, and a lot of good food.

Wind-farm early 1900's Style
Gary Wilhelm August 2019

Earlier this summer we were driving through southern Minnesota and saw a huge wind farm, with many large wind generators to provide power to the grid. This reminded me of my grandparent's farm in South Dakota, which also used wind power in the early 1900's, but with two, much smaller wind turbines: one to pump water for the farm, and the other to provide some electricity for their farmhouse.

My Wilhelm grandparents were Pennsylvania Dutch, and were located in Lancaster County, Pennsylvania. My father was the first of their six children, and was born there in 1906. In 1912, they boarded a train, with their few possessions and came to South Dakota. They were too late to get a free 160-acre piece of land if they would live on it for five years. However there were existing farms they could rent, which is what they did.

In 1943, I was my father's first-born surviving child and spent some time on their farm near Faulkton. The energy transformation I observed over the years there was remarkable. Initially they had two work horses (named Tom and Jerry) to do much of the farm work. They were big, very solid horses.

I am told that my father rode a different horse several miles to a one room country school.

All of the drinking water on the farm, was pumped by a wind-mill into a stock tank where the horses and cows could drink, too. There was a coffee can out at the stock tank which we would use to get a drink from the tank if we were thirsty. The coffee can was a little rusty, but oh well.

On top of the farm house was a wind charger, to provide some electricity. It charged a bank of lead acid batteries in the root cellar beneath the house. There was only enough electricity for several small lights to be on for a limited time at night. Electricity from the REA was not available until the early 1950's. Water for the house was carried in pails from the wind mill in the farm yard. The bathroom was an outhouse...a "two hole-er" located 50 or 100 feet from the house.

Heat for warmth and cooking was supplied by a large cast iron stove, which burned mainly corn cobs. In addition to the chickens, cattle, and pigs; food was grown in a large garden. In the fall, vegetables were canned for use in the winter. On the porch there was a wooden butter urn, and a "separator" for processing cream from raw milk.

Initially all of the energy was supplied by my grandparents, their work horses, and the wind. In my time, I do remember seeing a telephone. It was on a "party" land line. In the 1930's crops failed, and my grandparents could not make the payments on their farm. Fortunately New York Life allowed them to stay on the farm and rent it until they could buy it back as soon as crop yields improved. Eventually they purchased a diesel tractor for farming, and after decades of hard work on the farm, when they were 65 years old, they were able to retire and move to town and live quite comfortably.

I am struck by the changes I personally have seen in energy usage from my grandparent's farm, which for years, was pretty much "off the grid" and had minimal energy from the outside, at the beginning of the 20th century. As time passed, people used more and more fossil fuels to make life easier, but in the process jeopardized the planet.

I certainly am not advocating that all people should go back to small farms with windmills and horses. Today we have advanced wind energy, and solar panels that transform the sun's energy directly to electricity. We do need to make widespread changes, including use of renewable energy in order to conserve and protect our planet for the future.

Praise for Good Afternoon Vietnam: A Civilian in the Vietnam War
By Dr. Theodore Jerome Cohen

Gary Wilhelm hits it out of the park with his first-hand account of his work in RVN during the war.

Even though he was a civilian, parts of this story sound like they came directly from the television series M*A*S*H (which, of course, hearkens back to the Korean Police Action of the early 1950s). Wilhelm's trials and tribulations in performing his job (having to leave the country just to communicate with his company in the States? What was that about???!), much less the effort it took to perform the things we take for granted as we go about our daily lives (e.g., shopping), would have been enough to drive most people mad.

My hat's off to you, Gary; thank you for your service! What a great read. Anyone interested in what really went on behind the scenes during the war in RVN will not want to miss this book. It's a fast--and very enjoyable--read!

Five stars, all the way.

Find free curriculum for *Good Afternoon Vietnam* and *Alex Asks Grandpa About the Olden Days on the Wise Owl Factory* educational website.

Made in the USA
Columbia, SC
24 January 2021